CONTENTS

Do you live in the country or a town? Or perhaps you live in a city? Cities are places where large numbers of people live. Cities have usually developed over many years in areas where there are good access routes for transport, for example on the coast or by a river. They are often surrounded by agricultural land, or have developed near coal mines or other forms of industry.

New York lies beside two rivers and the Atlantic.

WHERE WE LIVE

By the year 2000, Mexico City will be the world's largest city, with more than 30 million people.

In the past, cities were self-sufficient – all the materials and food they needed came from the surrounding area. This area is called a city's 'footprint'. But as cities grew larger and world communications opened up, cities began to trade with other cities, and then with cities in other countries. Nowadays, a city's footprint is huge because most depend on a constant supply of goods from around the world.

Cities can spread long distances from the high-rise buildings of the centres to the suburbs.

CITY STRUCTURE

A typical city has a business and shopping centre with tall buildings, roads and little open space. Some people live in high-rise buildings near the centre. Others live further out in the suburbs. Industrial estates tend to be built outside the city, away from the residential areas, where large vehicles and trains can reach the factories more easily. Cities are linked by roads, railways and, in some cases, waterways. Basic services such as water and power supplies, drains and sewers have to be provided for millions of people.

Transport routes, such as train lines, keep cities alive, but also use up much open countryside.

Some of the world's largest cities are now home to more than 10 million people who live and work there.

THE MOVE TO THE CITY

As the world's population has grown, so has the number and size of its cities. The oldest cities date back almost 10,000 years. They were originally inhabited by just a few thousand people and surrounded by a wall for defence. Over the last few hundred years, there have been mass movements of people from the countryside to the cities, seeking jobs and a better way of life.

Old towns were often contained by a wall.

The world's population is growing rapidly. Today there are 5 billion people in the world, but within 25 years that number will rise to 8 billion. By then, more than half of the world's population will be living in towns and cities. If all these people are to be housed, our towns and cities are going to have to grow rapidly.

More people means the need for more resources.

EXPANDING CITIES

Cities are already expanding and the countryside is disappearing under new homes and roads. The extra people will also need more food, water and goods, all of which will have to be transported to the cities.

'By the turn of the century, the majority of the world's population will be living in cities.'

AGENDA 21

There will be more industry and the demands for energy will increase. Inevitably, there will be more waste to dispose of. All this means that city environments are going to be put under great pressure.

Much green space is lost to new buildings.

THE POOR NEED HOMES

Many cities are already experiencing problems caused by too many people. The poorest people often live in slums. These are areas in which people live crowded together in old buildings that are in desperate need of repair.

Every year the population of the city of New Delhi, India, increases by 600,000. The Chief City Minister of New Delhi said, 'By the year 2001, New Delhi will be the world's biggest slum.'

Millions of children in developing countries grow up in homes without water, drains or electricity.

Sometimes, shanty towns form on the outskirts of a city, often on land that is unsafe because it is too steep, or polluted, or in danger of flooding. Here, the poor have built their own makeshift shelters in areas which have been created without any planning. Thousands of people may live in tiny dwellings which lack any water supply, drainage or electricity supply. It is not surprising that disease spreads rapidly.

In Nairobi, Kenya, thousands of people live in rough shelters just a few metres from the homes of the rich.

How are we going to cope with all the extra city people without destroying the environment? This was one of the questions asked at the Earth Summit held in Rio de Janeiro, Brazil, in June 1992. People representing governments from around the world gathered to discuss the world's future.

The Tree of Life was the symbol of the Earth Summit.

ACTION PLAN FOR THE FUTURE

Agenda 21 is a huge document that was produced as a result of the Earth Summit. It is a practical action plan that looks at the problems facing the world and prepares us for the challenge ahead – surviving into the twenty-first century. It tries to find a way to create an acceptable lifestyle for all around the world, while protecting the environment so that future generations can live comfortable, healthy lifestyles, too.

The Earth Summit, or the United Nations Conference on Environment and Development, was the largest political meeting in history.

The issues raised in Agenda 21 focus on how we can protect our environment so we can continue to enjoy it.

'It is up to all of us to build on the foundations laid by the Earth Summit . . .'

Maurice Strong, author of the official publication of the Earth Summit.

We depend on our environment for the air we breathe, the water we drink, the food we eat and for the materials we use to build our homes and cities. Some of these resources cannot be expected to last forever. There has to be a balance between the needs of people and the environment.

We need to use resources, such as timber, carefully to make sure they last into the future.

If our environment is to be protected we all have to change our lifestyles. We must conserve and recycle resources and create as little waste and pollution as possible. The whole plan is called 'sustainable development'. A sustainable city is one that has a small footprint, using more local resources and relying less on imported goods from faraway places.

Recycling materials is a good way to conserve resources.

SUSTAINABLE CITIES

The action plan aims to improve the living and working environments of all people, especially the poor. This means less pollution and waste, cleaner streets and healthier living conditions.

'We need less luxury and waste in a few countries so there can be less poverty and hunger in a greater part of the world.'
Fidel Castro, President of Cuba, 1992.

There is a big divide between the world's rich developed countries and the poorer developing countries, but all cities create too much waste and pollution, harming the world's environment.

(Above and left) Much of the waste we generate across the world could be reduced, especially from luxury items that are very wasteful.

Big, industrialized cities use up many resources, such as coal and oil. These are non-renewable resources that cannot be replaced. Cities in developing countries have a different type of problem. Many of their inhabitants live in poverty and, in order to give them a better way of life, these cities need to use more raw materials and energy. But cities have to use more *renewable* resources, such as wood, and use energy from the sun and wind which will never run out.

Oil is a valuable and non-renewable fuel.

AGENDA 21

Here are some of the most important aims of Agenda 21 that relate to homes and cities:

- provide better homes for all
- improve town planning
- encourage the careful use of land
- improve water and sewage systems
- reduce waste and dispose of rubbish carefully
- promote better use of energy
- encourage environmentally sensitive transport systems
- promote a sustainable construction industry

CASE STUDY

MEXICO CITY, MEXICO

THE ISSUES AT STAKE

Mexico City is a city out of control. One-fifth of Mexico's entire population now lives in Mexico City. Every day, 1,000 people arrive seeking homes and jobs. The city faces huge environmental problems. There is a shortage of clean, safe water. Factories pump pollution into the air and waste into the rivers. There are more than 2.5 million vehicles clogging the streets of Mexico, adding to the air pollution and creating a hazy smog layer which lies over the city like a blanket. More than 10,000 tonnes of rubbish are produced every single day, of which a quarter remains uncollected, so piles of rubbish are just part of city life. Mexico City has to find ways of improving the quality of life for its millions of inhabitants.

A thick layer of smog hangs over Mexico City.

AGENDA 21 aims to:

- save energy
- make and use equipment that uses energy efficiently
- use alternative energy sources, especially sun, wind and water

Wind energy is a renewable resource.

FUELLING THE CITIES

Every day, cities around the world use huge amounts of energy for industry and business, and in homes.

The world's richest countries use 80% of the world's energy.

Looking at a city at night, it is easy to see just how much energy is wasted: light streams from empty office blocks, from brightly lit advertising signs and street lights. Huge industrialized cities are big consumers of energy. These cities have to find ways of cutting back on their energy spending.

'All energy sources will need to be used in ways that respect the atmosphere, human health and the environment as a whole.'

AGENDA 21

The bright lights of New York by night. Imagine how much energy could be saved by switching off these lights.

Developing countries have a different problem. In order to improve their standard of living, they need to use *more* energy, but, if they are not careful, this will cause more pollution. It costs a lot to build new power stations and put up electricity pylons and lines. The best way forward is to improve energy use and make use of renewable energy sources, especially solar (sun), wind and water power.

In remote parts of the world, such as Central Africa, there is no electricity supply. These solar panels trap the sun's energy to heat water for cooking and washing.

CASE STUDY

HAMBURG, GERMANY

SAVING ENERGY IN SCHOOLS

Many schools in Hamburg are taking part in a project called 'Fifty-fifty' to save energy and water. The schools can keep 50% of the money they save on their energy bills to spend as they like. The schools looked carefully at their energy use, especially the heating systems. Lots of energy saving schemes were put into action. Some were very simple, such as putting thermometers in classrooms to check on overheating, closing doors, and remembering to switch off lights and equipment when they were not in use. In the first year, heating costs fell by 9% (this amount of energy would heat 400 households for one year), electricity was down by 7% (the electricity used by 175 homes in one year) and water use was reduced by 12%.

Now, the schools have more money to spend on equipment and facilities. The scheme was so successful that many more schools in Germany have joined the project.

South-facing glass walls and glass ceilings make the most of natural light.

AGENDA 21 aims to:

- house as many people as possible
- find more money for housing
- stop the movement of people to the cities from the countryside

FINDING MORE HOMES

Today, there are one billion homeless people in the world. As the population continues to rise steeply, it is becoming more and more difficult to provide even the most basic housing.

LAND IS EXPENSIVE

Land tends to be expensive in and around cities because it is in short supply, especially near city centres. There is a demand for new land for industry, high cost housing, new businesses and shopping centres, new roads and parks. Poorer people cannot usually afford to buy even the smallest plot of land within cities, so they often settle on the surrounding land. This may be a valuable habitat such as a forest, a wetland or a marsh. Sometimes, shanty towns develop.

Shanty towns are unhealthy and cause further habitat loss and pollution as they expand.

City planners have to try to find some way of giving poorer people plots of land on which they can build their homes and grow food. They also need low cost building materials, which ideally come from the local area. But it is not just the giving of land. The new housing must be managed properly. This is the role of the United Nations Development Programme. It was set up to improve transport, water, sewage and power supplies in areas that need support so that more people can lead healthier lifestyles.

In Cuba, local people grow organic vegetables on waste land, making good use of land within the city itself.

STOPPING POVERTY WITHIN CITIES

People are a very important resource, yet in some of the fastest growing cities, half the population is unemployed. Large scale unemployment leads to large scale poverty – this is a worldwide problem. Governments need to encourage people to set up small businesses, for example, making and repairing goods, or selling food. One way to reduce poverty is to create more jobs.

These Bangladeshi women are part of a local basket-weaving project which gives people jobs and an income.

STOP THE MIGRATION TO THE CITIES

The move to the cities, and the increasing pressure on city facilities and resources, has been growing over the last 20 years, especially in the developing countries. More and more people are forced to leave rural areas. Perhaps there is too little land available, or machinery has replaced the farm labourer. Often land has been overworked and cannot be used any more, or a war has made the area unsafe. The rural poor think the cities offer a better way of life and, quite often, this is true. The cities have electricity, hospitals and schools, and easier access to water.

(Above) Lack of water in rural areas can be a problem, forcing many people to move to cities.

One way to stop the workers moving to the city is to improve the rural way of life. This can be achieved by creating jobs in rural areas (left).

In India, there are schemes to encourage village industries and to train village people in crafts, such as wood carving, weaving and pottery. People are offered cheap loans so that they can buy materials and machinery. Farmers have been shown ways to water their land, so more land can be used to grow crops. They are also taught new ways of farming.

Local employment helps to raise rural standards of living.

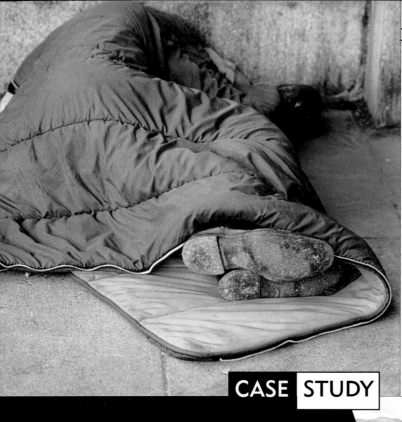

'All countries should take immediate measures to provide shelter to their homeless poor.'

AGENDA 21

Many people in the developed world sleep rough on the streets. Solutions need to be found so that every city provides adequate shelter for all its inhabitants.

CASE STUDY

CAJAMARCA, PERU

A PLAN FOR A CITY AND ITS SURROUNDS

Cajamarca City is surrounded by farmland. Many of the people of the city live in poverty. Their homes have no clean water, drains, sewers or electricity. These poor conditions affect the health of the people.

The action plan is in two parts. The first part aims to help farmers working the land around the city. They will be taught how to improve their land by terracing steep hillsides to stop the soil washing away, to plant tree nurseries, and to look after their animals. The second part will improve the city environment. There will be better rubbish collection, more parks and gardens, and trees in the streets. These improvements will cost a lot of money. Some of this money will come from the local mining companies whose mines pollute the local rivers. It will be their way of compensating the people for the damage the mines have done to the local environment.

Farmers in Peru are shown how to produce more food on their land.

AGENDA 21 aims to:

- provide more public transport
- build more cycle-ways and footpaths
- educate people about environmentally sensitive transport issues

NEW TRANSPORT SYSTEMS

The car dominates modern cities. Over the last 50 years, the number of cars has risen greatly, and the road networks cannot cope with the extra traffic. Heavy traffic leads to road accidents, noise, congestion and air pollution, all of which affect the health of the city people and the environment.

Effective transport is made more difficult by the steady expansion of the cities. The greater the sprawl, the greater the need to use the car to reach the workplace or the shopping centre.

The huge numbers of cars in and around cities such as Los Angeles create a layer of smog over the city.

PUBLIC TRANSPORT

One of the best ways of reducing traffic is to encourage people to use public transport – the buses, trams and trains. People often say that public transport is not as convenient as using their cars, or complain that it is badly run.

Local councils and city planners need to design transport systems that encourage people to jump on the bus rather than into their cars. The buses and trams have to be cheap to use, run frequently, and serve all the city areas. At the same time, city planners have to make it more difficult for car drivers, perhaps by charging them if they wish to reach the centre, or by making car parking very expensive. Just imagine how much more city space there would be if streets did not have car parking.

Trams serve all parts of the city of Zurich, making travel around the city easy and cheap.

RAPID TRANSIT SCHEMES

The tram, abandoned more than 50 years ago, is returning to European cities, such as Sheffield and Zurich. Modern trams are quiet, create little pollution and carry a lot of people in a small space, so they are very efficient people-movers.

Sydney's monorail runs on elevated tracks above the city.

Trams do need special rails in the road, however, which can make it difficult for other road users. In crowded cities, where there is little space, elevated tracks above the streets can be built instead.

CAR SHARING

Many of the cars on the road carry just one person, but it would be far more efficient and environmentally friendly if each car carried 3 or 4 people, since the amount of fuel used and pollution created is the same.

'The number of cars in the UK is growing by about 500,000 every year'

Transport 2000

In some cities, there are car sharing schemes. Cars taking part in the scheme have special lanes on the main roads which they alone can use, giving them quicker access to the city.

If people shared journeys, it would take some of the traffic off our already busy roads.

BAN THE CAR!

Some cities have banned the car completely. The streets are closed off to traffic – not only making it safer for people to walk through the centre, but making it more pleasant too.

'If I ruled the planet, I would introduce a car-free Sunday once a month. On this day, public transport would be free, or at least cheaper.'

Bettina Keuchel, aged 19, from Germany.

It is much more difficult, however, to ban the car in the suburbs. In an effort to reduce traffic in city centres, some cities do offer a 'park and ride' service where people are encouraged to leave their cars on the outskirts of the town and are taken into the centre by bus.

Caritiba, Brazil, has special lanes so buses can travel more quickly – to persuade people to use public transport.

LOW COST TRANSPORT

In many countries, the most common forms of transport are the bicycle, tricycle and rickshaw. These are simple vehicles which are cheap to buy and easy to run. They take up little space on the streets and, most importantly, are non-polluting. Often, they are made by local workers using local materials.

The three-wheeled, pedal-powered becak is common in Indonesia.

'Transport uses 60% of the world's consumption of oil.'

AGENDA 21

21

CASE STUDY

ERLANGEN, GERMANY

THE BICYCLE-FRIENDLY CITY

In the German city of Erlangen, bikes have priority over cars. Over the last 20 years, the city planners have encouraged people to use bikes or buses, or to walk, rather than use their car. They provided a network of bike lanes with a bike signpost system and city bike lane maps. Some bike paths are painted red so that they are clearly visible, and this helps at road junctions and stops car drivers parking their cars on them. Traffic lights are even programmed to allow cyclists to go first. Cyclists can also travel both ways on one-way streets and use streets barred to cars. All of these actions mean that it is easier to cycle round the city than to drive a car. It has been so successful that more than a quarter of the journeys made in the city are now made by bike — except in wet weather when people crowd on to the buses!

Some city authorities encourage cyclists by providing safe lanes and cycle-only areas.

AGENDA 21 aims to:

- provide people with clean water
- collect and dispose of rubbish in a safe and environmentally sensitive way
- dispose carefully of waste water and sewage

DISPOSING OF WASTE

DISPOSING OF WASTE WATER

Large numbers of people produce a lot of waste and need a constant supply of fresh, clean water. Dirty water and sewage must be treated before it is allowed to re-enter waterways. Water treatment can be expensive, so some cities look for other ways to deal with waste water.

In Calcutta, India, sewage is taken to a series of ponds outside the city. The sewage-filled water is moved from pond to pond, slowly getting cleaner. The sewage is broken down naturally by bacteria living in the water. Carp are kept in these ponds – these are fish which thrive in dirty water. So the ponds have two functions. They clean the water and provide local people with a cheap and plentiful source of fish.

The sewage ponds of Calcutta provide a good harvest of fish.

RECYCLING THE RUBBISH

Rubbish is also a pollution problem in cities. In the developed world, much waste ends up buried in landfill sites. Although recycling schemes exist, only about a fifth of the rubbish is recycled. This is a waste of both energy and resources. In some developing cities, waste has much more value. Local people sort through the rubbish by hand, looking for things which can be recycled, such as paper, metals and plastics. They take the valuable waste to factories and workshops where it can be used again.

Disposing of waste is a problem (above); sorting through for materials that can be recycled provides a living for some of the poorest people (right).

'By the year 2000, all countries must make sure that 75% of rubbish produced in urban areas is collected and recycled, or disposed of in an environmentally safe way.'

AGENDA 21

23

CASE STUDY

DAR ES SALAAM, TANZANIA

AN EMERGENCY CLEAN-UP OPERATION

Dar Es Salaam is a rapidly expanding city with many environmental problems. Raw sewage and factory waste pollute the local rivers and the sea. Rubbish lies uncollected on the streets or in illegal dumps. With the help of money from the United Nations, the city launched an emergency clean-up operation. Rubbish was cleared from the streets and taken to new, controlled landfill sites. Recycling schemes were set up for the local people. The city is now tackling its biggest environmental problem – water pollution.

Rubbish is taken to tips rather than being left on the streets.

AGENDA 21 aims to:

- use local materials wherever possible
- avoid using materials that can pollute, either in their mining or in their use
- encourage traditional methods of building construction
- encourage the building of energy-efficient houses
- help local employment by using labour intensive methods

Sand is a non-renewable resource.

BUILDING FOR THE FUTURE

Cities are man-made environments, created with concrete, tarmac, bricks and steel. All these have been made from raw materials, such as limestone, iron ore, sand and gravel. These are non-renewable resources. To preserve them, we have to be more careful about their use.

RECYCLING BUILDING MATERIALS

Cities change rapidly. Because of the high cost of land, unwanted or derelict buildings are quickly pulled down, the site cleared, and new buildings are erected. Far too often, the old building materials are dumped and fresh materials are used for the new building. The old materials could be recycled and used again.

If buildings were taken down carefully, the materials could be reused.

USING RENEWABLE BUILDING MATERIALS

It is possible to create buildings using materials from a renewable source. Better use can be made of natural fibres and wood, which can be grown in a sustainable way. When the trees are felled for timber, new trees must be planted in their place and, of course, it is important not to use more trees than the number being replanted. Crops of jute, flax and hemp provide strong natural fibres that are plentiful, cheap and renewable. These fibres can be woven into fabrics for use in buildings instead of plastic, or they can be packed between walls for insulation.

Fresh supplies of natural materials can be grown each year.

CASE STUDY

THE ENVIRONMENTALLY SENSITIVE HOUSE

An environmentally sensitive house can be just as comfortable to live in as a normal house. It may look very similar, but it has features that save energy and resources. Instead of using new bricks and tiles, the builder can use second-hand materials, recycled from buildings that have been demolished. Wood is a renewable resource and this is ideal to use for doors, window frames and floors. To reduce heat loss, the walls and roof can be insulated using special insulation made from recycled newspaper. Window size affects heat loss, so small windows are used on the north side of the house and large windows on the south side which gets more sun. Solar panels may be used to heat water and provide electricity.

The south-facing wall is made from glass to trap the sunlight.

STOP THE SPRAWL!

The oldest buildings within a town or city are found nearest the centre. As new shops and industrial estates appear on the outskirts of the city, the centres begin to get run down and shops and businesses close. In the USA, city centres are nicknamed doughnuts because there is nothing but a hole in the middle! New housing estates, even whole towns, are built on countryside outside the city. Then more roads are built so people can drive from their homes to offices and shopping malls. Soon the city loses its 'heart'.

URBAN RENEWAL

City centres need to be improved to bring life back to the centre. One way is to rebuild and repair the older buildings in order to create new business premises or homes. Alternatively, derelict buildings could be demolished and replaced with new houses or open spaces for recreation.

(Above and left)
City centres can be given new life by repairing or demolishing buildings that are run-down, replacing them with new buildings or attractive parks.

In the past, many cities built on rivers or coasts had docks: as ships became larger, the small city docks with their warehouses and factories fell into disuse. Nowadays, cities are redeveloping their docklands. Warehouses are converted into homes; shops and restaurants are developed along the waterfront and are popular with both residents and tourists.

'If I ruled the planet, I would ban all arms production and use the money saved to employ people to clean up polluted areas.'

Amandine Deguand, aged 17, from France.

In the future, urban renewal will play an increasingly important part in city development. Natural habitats everywhere are under threat so cities will not be able to continue increasing in size. Planners will have to look carefully at the use of land and find ways of using it more effectively.

Renovated areas help to bring life back to city docklands.

The modern city is very different to the towns and cities of the past. It is a mass of concrete and tarmac that sprawls over a huge area. Every day it uses up resources which are brought in from all over the world. We need to make our cities more environmentally sensitive and less dependent on new resources. Cities need to be more self-sufficient — they need to have as small a 'footprint' as possible.

PLANNING FOR THE FUTURE

Surveyors and town planners can help build environmentally sensitive cities for the future.

VOTING FOR CHANGE

When you are older, you will probably be entitled to vote. Most governments are put into power by people voting for them. People can get involved in local decision-making processes, too. Check out those who represent your city. Look at their plans for the city. Find out about your city's local Agenda 21. How does it plan to see your city into the 21st century?

A LIVING CITY

With careful planning, it is possible to make existing cities more environmentally sensitive. An amazing variety of wildlife can already be found living in cities. Derelict sites can be turned into nature reserves. It is also possible to create wildlife corridors which criss-cross the city, linking parks and making it easier for wildlife to move about.

(Above) As rural areas decrease, city wildlife may increase.

GREENPOINT, NEW YORK CITY

BECOMING INVOLVED IN THE FUTURE OF YOUR CITY

The people of Greenpoint were worried about pollution and wanted to see local industry working in as environmentally a sensitive way as possible. They have set up a Citizens' Advisory Committee (CAC) consisting of local people and environmental experts. Many projects are under way to improve recycling and reduce local pollution. The Clean and Green project has teams of people who tidy up local parks and plant trees and shrubs.

PARTNERSHIPS

Cities can be exciting places. They provide homes and jobs and offer many activities. We need to rebuild our city centres, to make the most of the resources that are already there. By limiting the need to travel away from the city centre, improving public transport, building up local employment and buying goods made locally, cities will become more self-sufficient. This does not mean that cities cannot still communicate globally.

29

Many cities have been 'twinned' with others elsewhere in the world. This arrangement can benefit both cities in the partnership. It gives the people of one city a chance to visit their twin city, to see how the other city works, and to exchange ideas. If the world is to develop in a sustainable way, it is vital that we learn from and support each other.

(Above) The people of Curitiba, Brazil, have worked hard to improve the natural areas in their city.

GLOSSARY

bacteria: tiny living cells which can be used to break down waste materials such as sewage.

derelict: describes buildings that are left unused and which gradually fall into ruin.

developed country: a country that relies on money from industry and in which factories provide more jobs than agriculture.

developing country: a country that relies on agriculture, rather than on manufacturing goods for export, for example.

export: to send goods out of a country.

government: a group of people, usually elected by the public, to run the country.

habitat: a plant's or animal's natural environment.

housing estate: a large area of housing.

import: to bring goods into a country.

industrialized: when a country's or city's income is based on the manufacturing and sale of goods.

industrial estate: land used for factories.

non-renewable: something that cannot be replaced; once a non-renewable resource, such as oil, is taken from the environment it is gone permanently.

pollution: harmful substances in the air, water or ground.

public transport: vehicles, such as buses, that anyone can use if they pay.

raw material: a material, or resource, that is in its natural state. For example, sand is a raw material that can be used to make cement.

renewable: something that can be replaced or regrown, for example trees, or a source of energy that never runs out, such as the sun or wind.

residential: where people live.

sewage: the solid waste from toilets which is carried away in the drains.

shanty town: an area on the edge of a town or city where people have built their own homes.

shopping centres: large area of shops with car parking usually provided.

slum: run-down buildings where people often live in overcrowded conditions.

suburb: an area of housing on the edge of a city.

sustainable: in this instance, to be able to maintain lifestyles or preserve resources over a long period of time.

traffic congestion: when traffic becomes too heavy to move freely.

urban development: the expansion of a city, or the addition of new areas to the city.

urban renewal: the rebuilding of part of a city or town.

FURTHER INFORMATION

Centre for Alternative Technology
Machynlleth
Powys, Wales, UK
Tel: 01654 702400

**European Sustainable Cities
and Towns Campaign**
Rue du Cornet 22B-1040
Brussels, BELGIUM
(Website http://www.iclei.org/europe)

**International Council for Local
Environmental Initiatives (ICLEI)**
(Website http://www.iclei.org)

Transport 2000
Walkden House
10 Melton Street
London, NW1 2EJ, UK

**United Nations
Environment Programme**
PO Box 30-22
Nairobi, Kenya,
EAST AFRICA

**Australian Nuclear Science and
Technology Organization**
New Illawarra Road
Lucas Heights, NSW 2234
Sydney, AUSTRALIA
Tel: 02 9717 3111

**Energy Information Centre
(Earth Exchange)**
18 Hickson Road
The Rocks, NSW 2000
Sydney, AUSTRALIA
Tel: 02 9247 1144

Environment Centre (NSW) Pty Ltd
39 George Street
Sydney, NSW 2000
AUSTRALIA
Tel: 02 9247 2228

State Research and Development
29 Christie Street
St. Leonards, NSW 2065
Sydney, AUSTRALIA
Tel: 02 9901 8888

INDEX